My First Acrostic

The South

Edited by Jenni Bannister

First published in Great Britain in 2011 by:

Young Writers

Remus House
Coltsfoot Drive
Peterborough
PE2 9BF
Telephone: 01733 890066
Website: www.youngwriters.co.uk

All Rights Reserved
© Copyright Contributors 2011
SB ISBN 978-0-85739-472-9

Foreword

The 'My First Acrostic' collection was developed by Young Writers specifically for Key Stage 1 children. The poetic form is simple, fun and gives the young poet a guideline to shape their ideas, yet at the same time leaves room for their imagination and creativity to begin to blossom.

Due to the young age of the entrants we have enjoyed rewarding their effort by including as many of the poems as possible. Our hope is that seeing their work in print will encourage the children to continue writing as they grow and develop their skills into our poets of tomorrow.

Young Writers was established in 1990 to nurture creativity in our children and young adults, to give them an interest in poetry and an outlet to express themselves. This latest collection will act as a milestone for the young poets and one that will be enjoyable to revisit again and again.

Contents

Caelan Landers (6) 1

Alexander Hosea Primary School, Wickwar
Daniel Cronin (6) 1
Scarlett Howes (6) 2
Jack Rawlins (6) 2
Cerys Forsdike (5) 3

Amesbury CE (VC) Primary School, Amesbury
Bronwen Medeiros (6) 3
Rhea Hulcoop (6) 4
Lewis Allen (7) 5
Callum Kealey (6) 6
Danny Sinclair (6) 7
Katie Hillier (7) 8
Ellie Gifford (6) 9
Lucy-May O'Sullivan (6) 10

Avondale School, Bulford
Matilda Heinrich (6) 10
Karl Callaway (7) 11
Honour Norman (6) 11
Llewellyn Evans (6) 12
Daisy Pullen (7) 12
Sophia Nicastro (6) 13
Fraser Doig (6) 13
James Robinson (7) 14
Max Glibbery (6) 14

Beechwood Primary School, Luton
Mehreen Khan (6) 15
Mathusha Sivakumaran (6) 15
Abdul Hussain (6) 16
Zuzanna Madon (7) 16
Hajra Haroon (6) 17
Richelle Bekoe (7) 17
Anika Dutta (6) 18
Hafsah Ali (6) 18
Hiba Haroon (6) 19
Kashaf Zahid (6) 19

Blackhorse Primary School, Emersons Green
Jessica Hembrough (4) 20
Harry Bradford (5) 21
Brooke Hussey (4) 21
Lucy Beresford (5) 22
Josie Murray (5) 23

Bourton on the Water Primary School, Bourton on the Water
Billy Richards (5) 24
Erika Creed (6) 24
Daisy Townsend (6) 25
Zachariah Vacher (5) 25
Ella Lainton (5) 26
Jed Sturge (5) 26
Jack Spence (5) 27
Jamie Baldwin (5) 27
Luke Daniels (6) 28
Huw Glyn Parry (5) 28
Katie Blanco (5) 29
George Whitley (6) 29
Rebecca Anderton (5) 30
Erin Butler (6) 30
Kai Jones (7) 31
Lex Goddard (5) 31
Tilly Arnell (5) 32
Ellie Burrows (6) 32
Alfie Rigby (6) 33
William Pulham (6) 33
Reece Oakey (6) 34
Euon Larner (7) 34
Oliver Tye (6) 35
Honey Kelly (6) 35
Teddy Halliday (7) 36
Kiyah Goodburn (6) 36
Libby Herbert (7) 37
Daniel Stroud (6) 37
Thomas Williamson (6) 38
Finley Harlow (6) 38
Marsha-May Townsend (7) 39
Tyla Morgan (7) 39
Tylor Wyatt (7) 40

Aaron Walters (6) 40	Joshua Collett (7) 61
Jacob Herbert (5) 41	Luke Dutch (7) 61
Ellie Dearman (5) 41	Charlotte Champion (7) 62
Jack Larner (5) 42	Lily Mills (7) 62
Reuben Morse (4) 42	Archie Gorton (7) 63
Oliver Castle (4) 43	Finlay Adamson (6) 63
Sophie Mitchell (4) 43	Conner Runyeard-Hunt (6) 64
Nicole Dos Santos (5) 44	Ben (6) 64
Aidan Thompson (5) 44	Daniel Hector (6) 65

Brightwell Cum Sotwell Primary School, Wallingford
Louis Wornham (6) 45
Henry Thorby (7) 45
Toby Bevis (6) 46

Drove Primary School, Swindon
Kirin Rue-Webb (7) 46
Madeleine Hutchinson (6) 47
Shirin Chaudhuri (6) 47
Yasin Khan (7) 48

Elm Grove Infant School, Littlehampton
Poppy Tester (7) 48
Libby Small (7) 49
Mollie Burford (6) 49
Matthew Cox (7) 50
Emma Bentley (7) 50
Matthew Horney (6) 51
Isabel Hunt (7) 51
Chloe Cooper (7) 52

Great Horwood CE Combined School, Great Horwood
Rianna Porter (7) 52

Grove Primary School, Trowbridge
Ben Noad (7) 53
Oliver Townsend (6) 53
Jack Thomas (7) 54
Emma Nohar (6) 55
Daniel Gardiner (7) 56
Milly Parsons (7) 56
Liam Parker (7) 57
Kieran Balchin (7) 58
Chelsea Latham-Coward (6) 59
Trinity Doyle (6) 59
Grace Kenny (6) 60

Kingscote School, Gerrards Cross
Henry Barnard (6) 65
Taran Glazebrook (7) 66
Thomas Bracken (7) 66
Nikolai Phillips (7) 67
Harry Brooks (7) 67
Thomas Guy (7) 68
Sebastian Los (7) 68
Nick Martin (7) 69
Archie Pritchard (6) 70
Munraj Bal (7) 70
Adam McDougall (7) 71
Noah Byrne (7) 71
Sebastian Jackson (6) 72
Oliver Gill (6) 72
Kuran Gosal (6) 73
Louis Causer (7) 73
Maxim Dusek (6) 74
Marcus Los (7) 75
Marcus Baines (7) 76

Luckwell Primary School, Bristol
Finn Setchell (5) 76
Cajsa Jonsson (5) 77
Luis Barry (5) 77
Julia Clarke (5) 78
Emily Turner (5) 78
Grace Flowers (5) 79
Phoebe Bullock (5) 79
Shelby Skidmore (6) 80
Molly King (5) 80
Elsie Rose-Carpenter (6) 81
Ethan Douglas (5) 81
Liam Brown (5) 82
Elif-May Kennedy (6) 82
Lucy Barnes (5) 83
Pierre Jones (6) 83

Leah Blatchford (6)	84
Aimee Ruck (6)	84
Joshkun Kennedy (7)	85
Milan Reed (6)	85
Thomas Yeo (7)	86
Oscar Vernon (7)	86
Jorja Rackstraw (6)	87
Lewis Lloyd (7)	87
Jack Buchanan (6)	88
Finlay Marsh (6)	89
Macy Pearce (6)	89
Nina Damian (6)	90
Jay Ramzan (7)	90
Lucy Nixon (7)	91
Milo Wood (6)	91
Cody Scragg (6)	92
Luke Ballard (6)	92
Lucy Anne Stone (7)	93
Emma Tatnall (7)	93

Millbrook Primary School, Freshbrook

Oliver Gargett (5)	94
Sam Moss (5)	94
Matthew Bowes (5)	95
Liam Hinton (5)	95
Harvey King (5)	96
Esmeralda Goodwin (5)	96
Charlotte Watson Boorman (6)	97
Ryan Gale-Wells (5)	97
Rachel Lewis (5)	98
Chloe Shailes (6)	98
Lauren Jones (6)	99
Molly Bannon (5)	99
Lewis Newcombe (5)	100
Tyler Thornbury (5)	100

Moorland Infant School, Beanhill

Danielle Winslow (7)	101
Martin Bailey (6)	101
Brodie Fyffe (7)	102
Angel Elliott (6)	103
Charlie Barfoot (6)	103
Chris Ete (7)	104
Kanica Rajanohan (6)	104
Misan Arubi (7)	105
Ebyan Abdullahi (6)	105

Norland Place School, London

Naomi Canny (7)	106
Elliot Hamilton-Croft (7)	106
Alexander Davies (7)	107
Caspar Presser Velder (7)	108
Alec Hogarth (7)	109
Jack Douglas (7)	110
Eva Strage (7)	111
Arun Mukherjee (7)	112
Oscar Jonhede (7)	113
Alicia De Broe-Ferguson (7)	114
Theo Mackenzie (7)	115
Alex Adams (7)	116
James Ward (7)	117
Isabella Chen (6)	118
Amelia Pearl (7)	119
Julia Baljé (7)	120

Stepping Stones Pre-Preparatory School, Froxfield

Lucia Harrison (6)	120
Tallulah Mackenzie-Smith (6)	121
Isabella Owen (6)	121
Amelie Summers (6)	122
Isabella Bidwell (5)	122
Charlotte Wordsworth (6)	123
Harry Markham (6)	123
Annabel Brown (6)	124
Edie Doherty (6)	124
Patrick Goodwin (7)	125
Jack McNally (6)	126
Jasper Fanshawe (7)	127
Phoebe Foxley (6)	128
Hugo Lawson (6)	129
Olivia Ashfield (7)	130

Stondon Lower School, Lower Stondon

Kelsey Ashby (5)	131
Toby Owen (6)	131
Luca La Francesca (5)	132
Cerys Fanning (7)	132
Dan Taylor (6)	133
Emily Surtees (6)	133
Cole Sugden	134
Robert Harrison (5)	134
Olivia Williamson (6)	135

Tom Edgecombe (6) 135
George Starling (6) 136
Jessamine Game (6) 136
Ashleigh Fenton (5) 137
Surena Kumar (6) 137
Kiera Marlow (6) 138

Whitefield Infant School, Luton
Nabilah Ibrahim (7) 138
Rayhan Ahmed (6) 139
Lauren Matear (7) 140
Ryan Chilvers (7) 141
Ashleigh Ridlington (6) 142

The Poems

My First Acrostic 2011 - The South

Grandad

Good old grandad.
Runs after the dog.
Annie's such a naughty girl.
No wonder Grandad gets out of breath.
Down dog, down!
After that Grandad needs a rest.
Down he lays for a doze.

Caelan Landers (6)

Silly Pig

Went to blow down the houses
Odd he is grey
Loves eating pigs
Feeling cross because he didn't eat a pig.

Daniel Cronin (6)
Alexander Hosea Primary School, Wickwar

Goldilocks And The Three Bears

G reedy for porridge
O dd because she broke into the bears' house
L onely because she couldn't find her way home
D oesn't help the bears
I n the bears' house
L ost in the woods
O nly eats porridge from bears
C ame through the back door
K ind of kind
S orry for the baby bear.

Scarlett Howes (6)
Alexander Hosea Primary School, Wickwar

Bad Wolf

W alking round the woods
O nly go near if you are brave
L et me go, don't eat me
F eeling scared.

Jack Rawlins (6)
Alexander Hosea Primary School, Wickwar

My First Acrostic 2011 - The South

Cinderella's Poem

C lever
I nteresting
N ice
D ancing
E ating
R ight
E xcited
L aughing
L ighting a candle
A way she went.

Cerys Forsdike (5)
Alexander Hosea Primary School, Wickwar

Bronwen

B rave because I like spiders.
R unning after my brother.
O ften I am shy.
N ice all the time.
W e are happy.
E ating all the time.
N ice, I am nice.

Bronwen Medeiros (6)
Amesbury CE (VC) Primary School, Amesbury

Rhea Hulcoop

R isky loves to sing.
H ooly loves to hoolahoop.
E lephant loves to stamp.
A lways knocks glasses off shelves.

H appy homework.
U gly hates birds.
L oves to dance.
C aring for my dog and puppy.
O h my work is hard!
O h I'm doing my work!
P inky loves pink.

Rhea Hulcoop (6)
Amesbury CE (VC) Primary School, Amesbury

My First Acrostic 2011 - The South

Lewis Allen

L aughing all the time.
E ats fish and chips.
W iggly wobbly.
I ce cream lover.
S illy Billy.

A mazing at work.
L ovely boy.
L istening a lot.
E ating a lot of the time.
N ot a chatterbox.

Lewis Allen (7)
Amesbury CE (VC) Primary School, Amesbury

Callum Kealey

C alming Callum is very, very hungry.
A lways happy as can be.
L oves playing on the computer.
L ikes to sing all the time.
U nique to everybody.
M unching on the best chocolate bar.

K ite flying is the best.
E ating all my tea up.
A mazing at running all the time.
L aughing all the time.
E xcellent at being still.
Y ummy things I like to eat.

Callum Kealey (6)
Amesbury CE (VC) Primary School, Amesbury

My First Acrostic 2011 - The South

Danny Sinclair

D angerous guy
A stonishing at rugby
N ot stupid
N ice chatterbox
Y ippity yappity

S illy boy
I ce cream lover
N ot silly
C learly not a girl
L aughing all the time
A mazing work
I 'm not stopped
R aving rabbits are fun to play with.

Danny Sinclair (6)
Amesbury CE (VC) Primary School, Amesbury

Katie Hillier

K atie is a good example to all her friends.
A ll the time she is kind to everyone.
T alented at writing.
I am amazing at playing with my DS.
E ating chocolate and sweets is fun.

H ates spiders and flies, bees and bugs.
I love playing with my friends and Rachel.
L ikes singing and dancing.
L ikes the colour blue.
I am outstanding to my little sister Amy.
E ating chocolate I love most.
R ubbish at silly boy games.

Katie Hillier (7)
Amesbury CE (VC) Primary School, Amesbury

My First Acrostic 2011 - The South

Ellie Gifford

E xcellent at the DS.
L ove watching my dad playing on the Xbox.
L ove helping my mum.
I nterested in science.
E xcellent at art.

G ood at football.
I nterested in topic.
F un and helpful.
F ootball fan.
O n the playground I play with my friend.
R eading is my favourite thing.
D ictionaries are good for me.

Ellie Gifford (6)
Amesbury CE (VC) Primary School, Amesbury

Lucy-May

L ovely Lucy loves dancing.
U gly Lucy loves swimming with a duck.
C onstantly I play with my sister.
Y ummy, my tummy is rumbling.

M ummy I love you.
A gain I kiss my mummy.
Y ummy, my mummy smells good.

Lucy-May O'Sullivan (6)
Amesbury CE (VC) Primary School, Amesbury

Jelly

J iggling on my spoon
E very mouthful delicious
L ooks scrummy
L ooks shiny
Y ummy, yummy in my tummy.

Matilda Heinrich (6)
Avondale School, Bulford

My First Acrostic 2011 - The South

Beetroot

B owls of beetroot
E at them hot
E at them cold
T asty with mash
R ound and red
O nly red food on my plate
O ften eaten by *me!*
T oo much and I go *pop!*

Karl Callaway (7)
Avondale School, Bulford

Pizza

P izza for tea
I n the oven
Z illions of ham
Z illions of pineapple
A pizza is yummy.

Honour Norman (6)
Avondale School, Bulford

Chocolate Sweet Chocolate

C urly Wurly yummy sweet chocolate

H oney chocolate sweet chocolate

O nly a bar a day

C urly chocolate

O nly a lovely smell in the sky

L unch is the home of chocolate

A really good bar of chocolate

T asty sweet, sweet chocolate

E at chocolate every day.

Llewellyn Evans (6)
Avondale School, Bulford

Steak

S hall I eat it all?

T asty every time

E at it rare

A bsolutely the best

K eep some for later.

Daisy Pullen (7)
Avondale School, Bulford

My First Acrostic 2011 - The South

Orange

O ranges are round
R ound as a ball
A nother orange please
N ext morning I will eat orange
G reat orange
E xciting orange.

Sophia Nicastro (6)
Avondale School, Bulford

Apple

A pples are juicy
P eople eat them lots of times
P ick them off the tree
L ooks shiny
E ating apples is healthy.

Fraser Doig (6)
Avondale School, Bulford

Gammon

G ive me 100 slices now!
A lways eat it
M outh-watering
M ost delicious meat
O ther meats are not good
N o foods are better than gammon.

James Robinson (7)
Avondale School, Bulford

Cereals

C oco Pops are my favourite
E very cereal I eat is tasty
R ice Krispies pop in my bowl
E very mouthful is delicious
A lways eat it for breakfast
L ast crumbs
S poon them up.

Max Glibbery (6)
Avondale School, Bulford

My First Acrostic 2011 - The South

Monkeys

M onkeys are cheeky!
O ranges they hate
N oise they love!
K icking they are good at
E lephants they are scared of!
Y oghurts they spill a lot!
S ometimes they are very moody.

Mehreen Khan (6)
Beechwood Primary School, Luton

Mathusha

M athusha likes skipping.
A lways happy and joyful.
T imes tables are my thing.
H ave nice friends.
U nderstanding and kind.
S miles like sunshine.
H elp at school.
A lways likes maths.

Mathusha Sivakumaran (6)
Beechwood Primary School, Luton

Chocolate

C hocolate is my favourite food

H obNobs have sweet chocolate on the top

O range chocolate is the best, I like it the most

C hocolate rabbits are big and yummy

O nly for the life of Nesquik

L ike it! Like it!

A bdul's friend is Mini Eggs

T he bowl is full of Coco Rocks

E y! That's my chocolate Crunchie, don't touch it.

Abdul Hussain (6)
Beechwood Primary School, Luton

Zuzanna

Z ooming around the playground!

U ses a brush to brush her hair.

Z ebra is my favourite animal.

A pples I hate a lot.

N aughty she is sometimes.

N auha is my best friend.

A nts I step on!

Zuzanna Madon (7)
Beechwood Primary School, Luton

My First Acrostic 2011 - The South

Elephants

E lephants eat a lot.
L ike to stomp around!
E at really messily!
P laying with the trees.
H ating little insects.
A pples are very juicy for them.
N ot even doing a lot of work.
T aking other people's stuff!
S tealing at night too!

Hajra Haroon (6)
Beechwood Primary School, Luton

Rabbit

R abbits are my favourite pets
A nd they like to crunch a lot
B ouncing all around
B ringing lots and lots of food into the cage!
I like to cuddle them sometimes
T hey are so cheeky!

Richelle Bekoe (7)
Beechwood Primary School, Luton

Hamnah

H amnah is my best friend
A nd she's always funny
M aths is her thing
N ever scared of anything
A lways bright and sunny
H appy all day.

Anika Dutta (6)
Beechwood Primary School, Luton

Hafsah

H afsah loves skipping double dutch
A nd likes doing karate
F amous singer is what I want to be
S inging is the best thing
A cting is also lovely
H anging out with my friend though is also great.

Hafsah Ali (6)
Beechwood Primary School, Luton

My First Acrostic 2011 - The South

Hiba

H ey I learn my splits
I have my sisters here as well
B allet I will do when I'm seven
A fter all I am the best!

Hiba Haroon (6)
Beechwood Primary School, Luton

Kashaf

K ashaf likes to be at school
A pples are her favourite fruit
S he makes the best banana cakes
H er jumper is the colour blue
A ctress she will be when she's 18
F ancy that for a change.

Kashaf Zahid (6)
Beechwood Primary School, Luton

All About Jess

J ess loves to dance
E gg and soldiers are so yummy
S inging is what I like to do
S ledging is such fun when it snows

H ome is where I like to be
E lla and Olivia are my friends
M ummy and Daddy love me very much
B illy is my friend
R unning around is what I like to do
O n holidays I like to stay in a caravan
U ncles I have many
G randma and Grandad make me giggle
H ughie and Casper are my pets.

Jessica Hembrough (4)
Blackhorse Primary School, Emersons Green

My First Acrostic 2011 - The South

Harry (About Me)

H elpful
A ctive
R eally happy
R eally good
Y ellow is my best colour.

Harry Bradford (5)
Blackhorse Primary School, Emersons Green

Bees Fly

B ee
R un
O ctopus
O n
K angaroo
E lephant.

Brooke Hussey (4)
Blackhorse Primary School, Emersons Green

Me And My Food

L ucy likes leeks
U m, not really
C arrots and peas
Y um-yum

B ananas are nice
E gg and soldiers too
R oast chicken is
E specially tasty
S tir
F ry
O r my favourite
R eally special dinner is
D addy's amazing chicken pie.

Lucy Beresford (5)
Blackhorse Primary School, Emersons Green

My First Acrostic 2011 - The South

Josie's Poem

J am sandwiches are my favourite
O n rainy days I watch TV
S ummer is my favourite season
I n October it's my birthday!
E very day I colour a picture

M y cat is called Barney
U nder my bed is where I like to hide
R eading books is fun
R oundabouts make me dizzy
A pples are my favourite fruit
Y ellow is the best colour.

Josie Murray (5)
Blackhorse Primary School, Emersons Green

Billy

B illy likes to build things
I n my bed I like to watch TV
L illy my friend likes to play
L illy also likes to go on the Wii
Y es please I do.

Billy Richards (5)
Bourton on the Water Primary School, Bourton on the Water

Erika

E veryone is nice
R ich
I like animals
K itKats are nice
A pples are my favourite.

Erika Creed (6)
Bourton on the Water Primary School, Bourton on the Water

Daisy

D ogs are my favourite
A nts tickle my arm
I love Haribo
S and is my favourite
Y ou can smile.

Daisy Townsend (6)
Bourton on the Water Primary School, Bourton on the Water

Zak

Z ebras have black and white stripes.
A pples are green and red.
K icking a ball is fun.

Zachariah Vacher (5)
Bourton on the Water Primary School, Bourton on the Water

Ella

E lephants are big

L ikes Lego

L ikes lollipops

A lways likes cats.

Ella Lainton (5)
Bourton on the Water Primary School, Bourton on the Water

Jed

J ed is in bed

E very morning I play on my DS

D ad is going to work.

Jed Sturge (5)
Bourton on the Water Primary School, Bourton on the Water

My First Acrostic 2011 - The South

Jack

J ack likes Japanese people
A pples are crunchy
C ats are funny
K icking a ball is fun.

Jack Spence (5)
Bourton on the Water Primary School, Bourton on the Water

Jamie

J am is my favourite
A man saw me doing some writing
M ammoths are my favourite
I am big
E very day I go swimming.

Jamie Baldwin (5)
Bourton on the Water Primary School, Bourton on the Water

Luke

L ego is great
U p! the movie
K icking a football
E very day I play the computer.

Luke Daniels (6)
Bourton on the Water Primary School, Bourton on the Water

Huw

H elpful
U p in the sky is the sun
W ater is wet.

Huw Glyn Parry (5)
Bourton on the Water Primary School, Bourton on the Water

My First Acrostic 2011 - The South

Katie

K ind
A pple
T iger
I like eating
E very night I watch TV.

Katie Blanco (5)
Bourton on the Water Primary School, Bourton on the Water

George

G irls
E veryone
O range
R unning
G oat
E lephants.

George Whitley (6)
Bourton on the Water Primary School, Bourton on the Water

Rebecca

R ebecca likes horses
E lephants are silly
B alls roll on the floor
E lephants have tails
C ats have tails
C ats have claws on their paws
A cat likes fish.

Rebecca Anderton (5)
Bourton on the Water Primary School, Bourton on the Water

Erin

E rin likes turtles, the ones who swim underwater
R escuing people
I like octopuses because they have eight legs
N oodles with tuna and cucumber.

Erin Butler (6)
Bourton on the Water Primary School, Bourton on the Water

My First Acrostic 2011 - The South

Kai Jones

K ites are my favourite thing.
A pples are my favourite fruit.
I am nice.

J oy - the lovely summer.
O range is a lovely colour.
N o I don't like yellow.
E veryone likes me.
S ometimes I am good.

Kai Jones (7)
Bourton on the Water Primary School, Bourton on the Water

Lex

L ex likes burgers
E veryone has friends
X -rays can look in your body.

Lex Goddard (5)
Bourton on the Water Primary School, Bourton on the Water

Tilly

T illy has a best friend
I like octopuses
L ikes Mrs Hourihan
L ikes lollipops
Y oghurts are yummy.

Tilly Arnell (5)
Bourton on the Water Primary School, Bourton on the Water

Ellie

E llie likes eating
L ying down
L iteracy is my favourite
I like rabbits
E very day I have a cup of tea.

Ellie Burrows (6)
Bourton on the Water Primary School, Bourton on the Water

My First Acrostic 2011 - The South

Alfie

A really fun boy
L ike a footballer I like white
F riends keep me company
I like football
E verybody likes me.

Alfie Rigby (6)
Bourton on the Water Primary School, Bourton on the Water

William

W rites perfectly
I nterested in tractors
L ove my teddies
L ove buses
I nterested in work
A dventurous
M y favourite game is football.

William Pulham (6)
Bourton on the Water Primary School, Bourton on the Water

Reece

R eady for work
E njoys playing football
E xcellent at football
C lever at homework
E veryone likes me.

Reece Oakey (6)
Bourton on the Water Primary School, Bourton on the Water

Euon

E njoy football.
U sually I am good.
O ften I am kind.
N ever naughty every week.

Euon Larner (7)
Bourton on the Water Primary School, Bourton on the Water

My First Acrostic 2011 - The South

Oliver Tye

O utside I play football
L ikes playing football
I think I am noisy sometimes
V ery good sometimes
E veryone likes me
R eady for work

T ries to do jobs to help Mum
Y ellow is not my favourite colour
E ggs are my favourite food.

Oliver Tye (6)
Bourton on the Water Primary School, Bourton on the Water

Honey

H ave lovely times.
O nce I went to the park.
N ever wear pink clothes.
E veryone likes me.
Y ellow is my favourite colour.

Honey Kelly (6)
Bourton on the Water Primary School, Bourton on the Water

Teddy

T oday I feel happy
E very day I drive to school
D on't like Power Rangers
D on't like pink
Y ellow is my favourite colour.

Teddy Halliday (7)
Bourton on the Water Primary School, Bourton on the Water

Kiyah

K ind and friendly
I ncredibly strong
Y ellow is not my favourite colour
A nd I can jump high
H appy and funny.

Kiyah Goodburn (6)
Bourton on the Water Primary School, Bourton on the Water

My First Acrostic 2011 - The South

Libby

L ollipops are my favourite treats.
I am a neat writer.
B utterflies are my favourite animals.
B alls are fun to play with.
Y ellow is my favourite colour.

Libby Herbert (7)
Bourton on the Water Primary School, Bourton on the Water

Daniel

D oesn't shout
A lways has battles
N ever loses a battle
I am a very good battler
E very day I am good
L oves to play.

Daniel Stroud (6)
Bourton on the Water Primary School, Bourton on the Water

Thomas

T om is playful.

H appy running around.

O ranges are juicy I like them.

M y friends like me.

A t the play pit I played.

S oup is yummy I like it.

Thomas Williamson (6)
Bourton on the Water Primary School, Bourton on the Water

Finley

F irst thing in the morning I have yummy breakfast

I am good at football

N ever nice to my brother

L ollies are one of my favourite things

E veryone loves me

Y ellow used to be my favourite colour.

Finley Harlow (6)
Bourton on the Water Primary School, Bourton on the Water

My First Acrostic 2011 - The South

Marsha May

M y favourite colour is purple.
A lways sensible in class.
R eady to write.
S weet and happy.
H opping is my favourite sport.
A t playtime I play with my friends.

M y favourite food is sweets!
A lways a good girl.
Y ellow used to be my favourite colour.

Marsha-May Townsend (7)
Bourton on the Water Primary School, Bourton on the Water

Tyla

T ea is one of my favourite drinks but hot chocolate is the best.
Y ellow is one of my favourite colours.
L earning is tiring and fun.
A n ice cream makes me as happy as can be.

Tyla Morgan (7)
Bourton on the Water Primary School, Bourton on the Water

Tylor

T elevision I watch every day
Y oghurt is yummy
L ike to be a little bit naughty
O utside on the climbing frame
R oast dinner is my favourite.

Tylor Wyatt (7)
Bourton on the Water Primary School, Bourton on the Water

Aaron

A really fun boy.
A lways nice.
R eally good at making friends.
O ften I am kind.
N ever lose a fight.

Aaron Walters (6)
Bourton on the Water Primary School, Bourton on the Water

My First Acrostic 2011 - The South

Jacob

J ay
A lbatross
C uckoo
O strich
B lack cap.

Jacob Herbert (5)
Bourton on the Water Primary School, Bourton on the Water

Ellie

E gg
L olly
L ion
I nk
E lephant.

Ellie Dearman (5)
Bourton on the Water Primary School, Bourton on the Water

Jack

J aguar
A pple
C at
K ittens.

Jack Larner (5)
Bourton on the Water Primary School, Bourton on the Water

Reuben

R abbit
E gg
U mbrella
B one
E nd
N est.

Reuben Morse (4)
Bourton on the Water Primary School, Bourton on the Water

My First Acrostic 2011 - The South

Oliver

O ranges
L olly
I ce Cream
V an
E lephant
R ed.

Oliver Castle (4)
Bourton on the Water Primary School, Bourton on the Water

Sophie

S nake
O ranges
P ig
H en
I nk
E gg.

Sophie Mitchell (4)
Bourton on the Water Primary School, Bourton on the Water

Nicole

N ut
I n
C lock
O liver
L ollies
E lephant.

Nicole Dos Santos (5)
Bourton on the Water Primary School, Bourton on the Water

Aidan

A idan likes apples
I love Daddy
D addy loves me
A idan likes toys
N oodles are yummy.

Aidan Thompson (5)
Bourton on the Water Primary School, Bourton on the Water

My First Acrostic 2011 - The South

North Pole

N orthern lights flashing
O ceans splashing on the shore
R eindeer being hunted by polar bears
T ired hunters coming back from hunting
H uskies pulling sledges

P olar bears eating baby seals
O bstacles floating on the water
L azy seals sunbathing on the shore
E lderly penguins waddling.

Louis Wornham (6)
Brightwell Cum Sotwell Primary School, Wallingford

Arctic

A rctic seals are swimming
R ound polar bears are swimming
C old and icy
T he polar bears are hunting
I nuits are catching their dinner
C ruel killer whales are hunting for their food.

Henry Thorby (7)
Brightwell Cum Sotwell Primary School, Wallingford

Arctic

A mazing big polar bears
R eindeer are flying in the dark
C old and freezing
T he polar bears are diving
I ce is very cold there
C old icebergs floating in the water.

Toby Bevis (6)
Brightwell Cum Sotwell Primary School, Wallingford

Extreme Sport

S aving
K issing the clouds
Y ellow parachute
D escending
I n the sky
V ery dangerous
E xercise.

Kirin Rue-Webb (7)
Drove Primary School, Swindon

My First Acrostic 2011 - The South

Extreme Sports

C unning climbers
L edge hanger
I ce caps
M ountains are rocky
B umpy rocks
I n the country
N ight climbing
G etting ready to start.

Madeleine Hutchinson (6)
Drove Primary School, Swindon

Extreme Sports

S uper girl
U p in the wave
R unning wave
F un sport
I n the wave
N o fear
G roovy adventure.

Shirin Chaudhuri (6)
Drove Primary School, Swindon

Extreme Sports

B reak down
I n the race
K nock out
I am a champion
N ight ride
G etting ready.

Yasin Khan (7)
Drove Primary School, Swindon

Winter Is Fun

W andering snowflakes
I n the snow
N ot a lot of sun
T hunder and lightning is loud
E veryone playing in the snow
R aindrops falling all around.

Poppy Tester (7)
Elm Grove Infant School, Littlehampton

My First Acrostic 2011 - The South

Winter

W inter has snow
I n the snow you can make a snowman
N asty weather
T ime to celebrate for Christmas
E xtremely cold and windy
R eally, really cold.

Libby Small (7)
Elm Grove Infant School, Littlehampton

My Brother

K ieran is very kind.
I n winter he stays at home.
E very day he plays on his DS.
R uns as fast as me.
A wesome person to have as a brother.
N oisy and shouty!

Mollie Burford (6)
Elm Grove Infant School, Littlehampton

Winter

W et and windy weather
I cicles are hanging from houses
N asty weather all the time in winter
T hunder and lightning is noisy
E verybody is in the snow
R aindrops are on your umbrella.

Matthew Cox (7)
Elm Grove Infant School, Littlehampton

Weather

W indy and cold weather
E veryone loves the snow
A utumn leaves are falling
T hunder and lightning is loud
H orrible hailstones hurt
E veryone loves summer holidays
R aindrops run down the window.

Emma Bentley (7)
Elm Grove Infant School, Littlehampton

My First Acrostic 2011 - The South

Weather

Weather is bad
Everyone loves some hot weather
All the wet weather is not nice
The cold weather is freezing
Hate the bad weather
Every season is different
Rain pours down like cats and dogs.

Matthew Horney (6)
Elm Grove Infant School, Littlehampton

My Brother

Finlay is a lovely brother
I love him
Naughty sometimes
Lovely other times
Always a pain
You and me together.

Isabel Hunt (7)
Elm Grove Infant School, Littlehampton

My Brother

C allum is funny and joyful

A ll Callum is interested in is the DS

L ovely and annoying brother

L oves his best, best friends

U sed to be lazy

M um and Dad love him.

Chloe Cooper (7)
Elm Grove Infant School, Littlehampton

Rianna

R eads a lot of books at home

I ncredible

A lways kind

N ice

N osey

A lways nice for friends.

Rianna Porter (7)
Great Horwood CE Combined School, Great Horwood

My First Acrostic 2011 - The South

Ben Noad The Brilliant Boy

B ubbly
E njoys school
N oisy

N ever nasty
O ften chatty
A lways kind
D oes good work.

Ben Noad (7)
Grove Primary School, Trowbridge

My Poem

O nly likes red
L ikes peas
I s happy
V ery helpful
E njoys making things
R eally fast.

Oliver Townsend (6)
Grove Primary School, Trowbridge

My Poem

J okes
A lways helps
C ares about people
K ind

T errific
H appy
O ften cheerful
M aths
A t home I help
S ays funny jokes.

Jack Thomas (7)
Grove Primary School, Trowbridge

All About Me

E very day the smiles

M akes butterflies

M usic

A lways happy

N ever stops working

O nly likes playing with her friends

H elpful

A lways kind

R uns fast.

Emma Nohar (6)
Grove Primary School, Trowbridge

Daniel

D on't like getting cold
A nd likes football
N ever gets grumpy
I s happy
E njoys PE
L ikes chips.

Daniel Gardiner (7)
Grove Primary School, Trowbridge

My Poem

M aking clay
I like maths
L oves PE
L oves our topic
Y awns a lot.

Milly Parsons (7)
Grove Primary School, Trowbridge

Liam Parker

L ikes to do clay.
I like to help Phoebe.
A lways likes to help my friends.
M akes people laugh.

P lays games.
A lways likes topics.
R eads books.
K ind.
E njoys school.
R uns fast.

Liam Parker (7)
Grove Primary School, Trowbridge

All About Me

K icking a ball is easy
I 've got small writing
E xcellent at spellings
R uns so fast
A lways being cheerful
N ever ever cries

B rilliant at reading
A lways enjoys outdoor PE
L ove to do literacy
C orrect nearly all my spellings
H appy all the time
I play with my friends
N ever gives up.

Kieran Balchin (7)
Grove Primary School, Trowbridge

My First Acrostic 2011 - The South

My Poem

C heerful
H appy
E xcellent
L oveable
S ensible
E njoys art
A lways kind.

Chelsea Latham-Coward (6)
Grove Primary School, Trowbridge

My Poem

T akes care of friends.
R eally kind.
I s helpful.
N ice.
I nteresting.
T ries her best.
Y awns a lot.

Trinity Doyle (6)
Grove Primary School, Trowbridge

Grace

G reat
R uns fast
A lways
C an do spellings
E xciting

K ind
E veryone's friend
N ice
N ever sad
Y is the last letter in Kenny.

Grace Kenny (6)
Grove Primary School, Trowbridge

My First Acrostic 2011 - The South

Joshua

J ealous I am

O utgoing

S ad

H appy

U ntidy

A mazing.

Joshua Collett (7)
Grove Primary School, Trowbridge

Luke

L ucky because I have 74p.

U ntidy because I never tidy my room.

K ind because I help others.

E xciting because I have exciting parties.

Luke Dutch (7)
Grove Primary School, Trowbridge

Charlotte

C razy.
H appy.
A chieves a lot.
R eally helpful.
L aughs a lot.
O utstanding.
T errific.
T alented.
E xcited.

Charlotte Champion (7)
Grove Primary School, Trowbridge

Lily

L ovely
I nteresting
L ikes laughing
Y ummy.

Lily Mills (7)
Grove Primary School, Trowbridge

My First Acrostic 2011 - The South

Archie

A mazing
R eally funny
C ool
H appy
I nteresting
E nergetic.

Archie Gorton (7)
Grove Primary School, Trowbridge

Finlay

F unny fun
I ncredibly nice
N ice and kind
L ucky and cool
A mazing
Y ummy.

Finlay Adamson (6)
Grove Primary School, Trowbridge

63

Conner

C razy
O riginal
N ice and helpful to others
N ice
E xtreme
R uins nothing.

Conner Runyeard-Hunt (6)
Grove Primary School, Trowbridge

Ben

B rave and fast
E very day I am good
N ice and helpful.

Ben (6)
Grove Primary School, Trowbridge

My First Acrostic 2011 - The South

Daniel

D aring
A mazing
N ice
I nteresting
E xcellent
L ovely.

Daniel Hector (6)
Grove Primary School, Trowbridge

Mr Fox

M r Fox has four children,
R abbit is Mr Fox's friend,

F antastic Mr Fox's family live in a hole,
O nce the farmers went to dig his family out of their home,
X mas turkeys were not used in the great feast.

Henry Barnard (6)
Kingscote School, Gerrards Cross

Henry

H enry was horrid,
E ven his parents were mean to him,
N ow his brother Peter was perfect,
R eading time,' said Dad,
Y ou're so horrid, Henry,' said Mum.

Taran Glazebrook (7)
Kingscote School, Gerrards Cross

Charlie

C harlie found a very, very shiny golden ticket.
H is aunts and uncles all sleep in the same bed.
A t the shop he bought a chocolate bar.
R an home excited.
L uscious bits of fudge.
I t was very yummy so he wanted more chocolate.
E agerly he ate the yummy scrummy bar.

Thomas Bracken (7)
Kingscote School, Gerrards Cross

My First Acrostic 2011 - The South

Charlie

C harlie was walking back from school when he found a dollar,
H e bought a chocolate bar,
A nd he got a golden ticket,
R eally spoilt children got sorted out by Willy Wonka,
L ovely chocolate river,
I t was a yummy chocolate factory,
E very child was spoilt except Charlie.

Nikolai Phillips (7)
Kingscote School, Gerrards Cross

Harry

H arry Potter was a wizard and he had a wand,
A lso he had a magic broomstick,
R an through the wall on platform 9¾,
R onald Weasley had ginger hair,
Y oung Harry had a scar on his head.

Harry Brooks (7)
Kingscote School, Gerrards Cross

The BFG

The BFG is ginormous,

He is a giant,

Even his ears were as big as his face,

Bottles of dream dust belonged to the BFG,

Friendly giant tried to stop the nasty giants,

Gently the BFG picked up Sophie very carefully.

Thomas Guy (7)
Kingscote School, Gerrards Cross

Preston

Pigs talk to Preston the pig,

Rude Mr Wolf tried to eat Preston the pig,

Each time Mr Wolf tried to get Preston the pig he missed,

School teachers help us to read books,

The pigs are very sneaky,

One of the pigs never gets caught by Mr Wolf,

Nick is Preston the pig in our assembly.

Sebastian Los (7)
Kingscote School, Gerrards Cross

Horrid Henry

H enry has a brother called Perfect Peter,
O nce he pinched Peter,
R alph is Horrid Henry's best friend,
R eally, Horrid Henry hates Margaret,
I love Henry B but I don't like Horrid Henry,
D inner restaurants were a nightmare for Henry,

H enry's mum and dad are horrid,
E ach day Horrid Henry would do something bad,
N ow Margaret is called a bossy boots sometimes,
R alph likes to play tricks on people,
Y ou would like to look at a Horrid Henry book.

Nick Martin (7)
Kingscote School, Gerrards Cross

Peter Pan

P eter Pan came to Wendy's house,
E ach person loved flying,
T hen Peter took Wendy to Neverland,
E very Lost Boy wanted Wendy to be their mum,
R ed Indians sowed Teddy together,

P eter Pan defeated Captain Hook,
A ll the lost boys went back with Wendy,
N obody got lost.

Archie Pritchard (6)
Kingscote School, Gerrards Cross

Henry

H orrid Henry was a horrid boy, he pinched Peter.
E ach time he pinched Peter he screamed, 'Mum, Henry pinched me.'
N ot now, I'm busy,' said Mum. 'But Henry's calling me names.'
R eading is horrible,' said Henry.
Y ou are horrid Henry, go to your room.'

Munraj Bal (7)
Kingscote School, Gerrards Cross

A Roald Dahl Poem

There once lived a big giant,
He had a friendly nature,
Ears were ginormous,

Big brown sandals he wore,
Friends with a girl,
Great friend to have.

Adam McDougall (7)
Kingscote School, Gerrards Cross

A Roald Dahl Poem

Matilda was a marvellous girl,
And her parents not so much,
Tremendously clever Matilda was,
In the house Matilda read,
Lying on her bed,
Determined to get more books,
And she deserves them too!

Noah Byrne (7)
Kingscote School, Gerrards Cross

A Roald Dahl Poem

J ames is a poor boy,
A nd his aunts are horrid,
M aybe James had lost it,
E veryone knows the aunts are horrid,
S o the bugs helped him.

Sebastian Jackson (6)
Kingscote School, Gerrards Cross

A Roald Dahl Poem

J ames had a sad life,
A bad thing happened to James,
M um and Dad died,
E arthworm was not very nice,
S ee James was a fantastic boy.

Oliver Gill (6)
Kingscote School, Gerrards Cross

A Roald Dahl Poem

T he BFG was a big-eared giant,
H e was so friendly,
E very dream he bottled up,

B ig-hearted giant,
F riends with a girl,
G reat, amazing giant!

Kuran Gosal (6)
Kingscote School, Gerrards Cross

A Roald Dahl Poem

T he Twits play naughty tricks on each other,
W icked horrible Twits,
I n a cage they kept monkeys,
T errible things they did to the monkeys,
S o the monkeys tricked them.

Louis Causer (7)
Kingscote School, Gerrards Cross

A Roald Dahl Poem

Willy Wonka owns the entire factory,
 I think he is clever and funny,
 Lives in a chocolate factory,
 Likes a bed made of chocolate,
 Yikes, Augustus Gloop, a fat nincompoop!

Wow, Augustus Gloop is infantile,
 Oh, what a greedy brute and louse's ear,
 No, no, no! Augustus Gloop is greedy,
 Know Augustus Gloop?
 Augustus Gloop is a nincompoop!

Maxim Dusek (6)
Kingscote School, Gerrards Cross

A Roald Dahl Poem

M uggle Wump is a fantastic monkey,
U pside down monkey,
G o to Africa with Roly Poly Bird,
G lorious clever monkey,
L eave the furniture on the ceiling,
E ndless amazing monkey,

W here will they put the furniture?
U gly Twits they will trick,
M uggle Wump is very clever,
P ut a trick on the Twits.

Marcus Los (7)
Kingscote School, Gerrards Cross

A Roald Dahl Poem

T he Twits have dirty habits,
H airy Mr Twit is ugly, very ugly,
E very sort of food in his beard,

T he Twits played tricks on each other,
W hen Mrs Twit has a glass eye,
I t is good to play tricks,
T he Twits have bird pie,
S o the book is excellent.

Marcus Baines (7)
Kingscote School, Gerrards Cross

Finn

F ine
I love
N ice
N ever hit.

Finn Setchell (5)
Luckwell Primary School, Bristol

My First Acrostic 2011 - The South

Cajsa

C at girl
A t Bristol
J olly girl
S mashing
A mazing.

Cajsa Jonsson (5)
Luckwell Primary School, Bristol

Luis

L ove
U nhappy
I n class
S illy.

Luis Barry (5)
Luckwell Primary School, Bristol

Julia

J ulia is nice
U sually happy
L ike my mum
I like them
A mazing.

Julia Clarke (5)
Luckwell Primary School, Bristol

Emily

E xtra nice
M um I like
I like elephants
L ove to be good
Y es, I am happy.

Emily Turner (5)
Luckwell Primary School, Bristol

My First Acrostic 2011 - The South

Grace

G reat
R ight
A pples
C risps
E ggs I like.

Grace Flowers (5)
Luckwell Primary School, Bristol

Phoebe

P retty
H airy
h O nest
E xcited
B ig children
E xcited.

Phoebe Bullock (5)
Luckwell Primary School, Bristol

Shelby

S ensible
H appy
E xcited
L ovely
B est
Y o-yo.

Shelby Skidmore (6)
Luckwell Primary School, Bristol

Molly

M onkey
O n the train
L ive in a house
L ittle
Y o-yo.

Molly King (5)
Luckwell Primary School, Bristol

My First Acrostic 2011 - The South

Elsie

E ngland
L ovely
S leepy
I am sweet
E ngland.

Elsie Rose-Carpenter (6)
Luckwell Primary School, Bristol

Ethan

E xcited
T op of the table are Man United
H appy
A B C
N ice.

Ethan Douglas (5)
Luckwell Primary School, Bristol

Liam

L ovely
I am weak
A rmadillo
M onkey.

Liam Brown (5)
Luckwell Primary School, Bristol

Elif

E veryone likes me
L ovely
I am excited
F riendly.

Elif-May Kennedy (6)
Luckwell Primary School, Bristol

My First Acrostic 2011 - The South

Lucy

L ovely
U mbrella bird
C ycling
Y um yums I love.

Lucy Barnes (5)
Luckwell Primary School, Bristol

Pierre

P ierre is a monkey
I am happy
E xcited
R obot
R hino
E xcited.

Pierre Jones (6)
Luckwell Primary School, Bristol

Leah

L ovely
E xcited
A pples, I like them
H air.

Leah Blatchford (6)
Luckwell Primary School, Bristol

Aimee

A lovely girl
I love her
M aking good
E veryone likes her
E veryone likes her.

Aimee Ruck (6)
Luckwell Primary School, Bristol

My First Acrostic 2011 - The South

My Name Is . . .

J umping on my mum's sofa.
O n Saturday I go to football training.
S undays I go to Hergrove Park.
H olidays in Cyprus.
K ick-ups are my favourite skill.
U nhappy when I fall over in the playground.
N ice to my beautiful sister, Elif.

Joshkun Kennedy (7)
Luckwell Primary School, Bristol

Milan

M onkey
I am excited
L ove
A t Bristol
N ice.

Milan Reed (6)
Luckwell Primary School, Bristol

My Name Is...

T om is a good pupil
H andy helper
O scar is my super-duper friend
M onster in the morning
A lways incredible
S ecret weapon in football

Y elling at my sister
E xcellent at sports
O n the football pitch all day.

Thomas Yeo (7)
Luckwell Primary School, Bristol

My Name Is...

O range is my favourite colour
S its around playing on my DS
C an do math sums very quickly
A lways prepared
R eady for anything.

Oscar Vernon (7)
Luckwell Primary School, Bristol

My First Acrostic 2011 - The South

My Name Is...

J anie is my favourite cat.
O n my birthday I play with my funny toys.
R ide my scooter home from school.
J umping on my trampoline.
A fter school I watch TV on my couch.

Jorja Rackstraw (6)
Luckwell Primary School, Bristol

My Name Is...

L ewis loves sports.
E xcellent at football.
W illiam is my friend.
I love rugby.
S aturday I play a match at Ashton Boys.

Lewis Lloyd (7)
Luckwell Primary School, Bristol

My Name Is . . .

J umping Jack
A ctive
C ool
K eeping the class tidy

B usy most of the time
U nder the weather sometimes
C hasing and dancing really well
H aving a good time all the time
A cting is fun
N ever naughty
A lways smiling
N ice all of the time.

Jack Buchanan (6)
Luckwell Primary School, Bristol

My First Acrostic 2011 - The South

My Name Is...

F inn's favourite food is ice cream
I like Ollie
N ice every day, never tidy my room
L ovely mum
A ugust is my birthday
Y ellow is my favourite colour.

Finlay Marsh (6)
Luckwell Primary School, Bristol

My Name Is...

M acy loves making jelly.
A lways play in my room.
C ats are my favourite animal.
Y ellow is my fourth favourite colour.

Macy Pearce (6)
Luckwell Primary School, Bristol

My Name Is...

N ice every day
I s good at swimming
N ever shout at my sister Christine
A pple is my third favourite fruit

D addy plays with me
A lways making things for my cat
M y favourite colour is purple
I love my sister Christine
A lways caring about my cat
N ice to my cat.

Nina Damian (6)
Luckwell Primary School, Bristol

My Name Is...

J acob, Luke and Rhys are my friends
A pples are my favourite fruit
Y ellow is my favourite colour.

Jay Ramzan (7)
Luckwell Primary School, Bristol

My First Acrostic 2011 - The South

My Name Is . . .

L ike lollipops
U mbrellas
C olourful
Y ellow is my fourth favourite colour.

Lucy Nixon (7)
Luckwell Primary School, Bristol

My Name Is . . .

M y favourite colour is red
I ce lollies are my favourite food
L ove swimming at Portishead on a Sunday
O n Tuesdays I go to Beavers.

Milo Wood (6)
Luckwell Primary School, Bristol

My Name Is . . .

C olourful bedroom.
O n Saturdays I go to dance.
D ad is annoying!
Y elling at Chad!

S hy.
H uggable.
E xciting.
Y ellow hair.

Cody Scragg (6)
Luckwell Primary School, Bristol

My Name Is . . .

L ove to play on my DS
U nusual things happen to me
K icking footballs in the net
E very weekend I visit my nanny.

Luke Ballard (6)
Luckwell Primary School, Bristol

My First Acrostic 2011 - The South

My Name Is . . .

L ove my two sisters.
U seful.
C olourful.
Y ellow hair for Lucy.

A ctive every day.
N ice every day.
N ow I'm doing hard work.
E xtra good at keeping things clean.

Lucy Anne Stone (7)
Luckwell Primary School, Bristol

My Name Is . . .

E very day I play Xbox
M y sister Danni is nice
M y favourite colour is red
A t bedtime I cuddle up with my teddies.

Emma Tatnall (7)
Luckwell Primary School, Bristol

I Am Oliver

O riginal
L ove
I ncredible
V ibrant
E nergy
R ock.

Oliver Gargett (5)
Millbrook Primary School, Freshbrook

Space

S pace is dark
P luto
A stronaut
C raters on the moon
E xplore the moon.

Sam Moss (5)
Millbrook Primary School, Freshbrook

Marvellous Matthew

M arvellous
A t the weekend I played football
T reat myself all day
T remendous
H appy
E veryone in my house says I am happy
W akes up early.

Matthew Bowes (5)
Millbrook Primary School, Freshbrook

All About Me

L iam is good at reading
I nterested in football
A m good at climbing trees
M atthew is my friend.

Liam Hinton (5)
Millbrook Primary School, Freshbrook

My Name Is Harvey

H arvey is brilliant.

A good ice skater.

R uns fast.

V ery good at maths.

E at an apple every day.

Y esterday I played football.

Harvey King (5)
Millbrook Primary School, Freshbrook

Darkness Of Space

D usty is the moon

A stronauts go to the moon

R ockets go in space

K ind aliens.

Esmeralda Goodwin (5)
Millbrook Primary School, Freshbrook

My First Acrostic 2011 - The South

Caring Charlotte

C harlotte is caring.
H aving a good time with my friends.
A lways having accidents.
R abbits are great.
L istening to my teacher.
O ranges are my favourite.
T omatoes are my very favourite.
T uesday is my favourite day.
E xcellent at reading.

Charlotte Watson Boorman (6)
Millbrook Primary School, Freshbrook

Space

S pace has planets
P lanets are great
A great space
C raters in space
E asy to go to space.

Ryan Gale-Wells (5)
Millbrook Primary School, Freshbrook

Really Cool Rachel

R eally cool Rachel
A mazing
C lever
H appy
E asy
L ovely.

Rachel Lewis (5)
Millbrook Primary School, Freshbrook

All About Me

C hain
H appy
L ooking good
O ats in porridge
E xcellent.

Chloe Shailes (6)
Millbrook Primary School, Freshbrook

My First Acrostic 2011 - The South

Lovely Lauren

L ovely
A mazing
U seful
R adical
E asy
N ice.

Lauren Jones (6)
Millbrook Primary School, Freshbrook

All About Me

M olly is nice
O bservant
L istening good
L ovely at writing
Y oung at bedtime.

Molly Bannon (5)
Millbrook Primary School, Freshbrook

Space

S pace is in the dark
P eaceful
A stronaut in space
C raters on the moon
E xplore the moon.

Lewis Newcombe (5)
Millbrook Primary School, Freshbrook

All About Tyler

T yler is nice
Y ou're good at reading
L ook at me
E xcellent
R ed and orange hair.

Tyler Thornbury (5)
Millbrook Primary School, Freshbrook

Carrot - My Favourite Vegetable

C runchy and healthy
A sleep in the ground
R ip them out
R eady to eat
O range and pointy
T otally delicious.

Danielle Winslow (7)
Moorland Infant School, Beanhill

Mango Is My Favourite Fruit

M um will put them in
A dish
N ibble it
G obble it
O h, it's good.

Martin Bailey (6)
Moorland Infant School, Beanhill

Strawberries - My Favourite Fruit

S weet and juicy
T aste like sugar
R ed and green
A nts nibble on them
W ash your hands
B ite them
E at them
R oll them in sugar
R oll them in cream
I have them with hot melted chocolate
E njoy the
S ugar on my lips.

Brodie Fyffe (7)
Moorland Infant School, Beanhill

My First Acrostic 2011 - The South

Grapes - My Favourite Fruit

G rapes are juicy
R ed like strawberry
A nd round and plump
P ut yummy grapes in
E at them all up
S orry all gone.

Angel Elliott (6)
Moorland Infant School, Beanhill

Apples Are My Favourite Fruit

A pples are red and juicy
P ink and bright, yellow and green
P inker than a flower
L et me fall, then
E at me!

Charlie Barfoot (6)
Moorland Infant School, Beanhill

Pineapple - My Favourite Fruit

P ineapples are sweet
I like pineapples
N ice pineapples
E njoy your pineapples
A nd you can drink pineapple juice
P ineapples are healthy
P ineapples are yummy
L ovely pineapples
E at the pineapples.

Chris Ete (7)
Moorland Infant School, Beanhill

My Favourite Fruit - Apples

A pple, red and juicy
P ick an apple
P ut it in your mouth
L ovely and sweet
E at it.

Kanica Rajanohan (6)
Moorland Infant School, Beanhill

Raspberry - My Favourite Fruit

R uby red
A nd eat
S weet
P retty
B eautiful
E at that
R ipe
R eady to eat
Y ummy.

Misan Arubi (7)
Moorland Infant School, Beanhill

Mango - My Favourite Fruit

M ango is yummy
A nd
N ice to eat
G ood and juicy like
O ranges now to eat.

Ebyan Abdullahi (6)
Moorland Infant School, Beanhill

Naomi

N aomi loves lovely lollipops that are sweet
A nd also I love bangers and mash, that's what I like to eat
O h, playing on my DSi is fun, that's what I like to do
M y favourite drink is lemonade especially if it's my mommy's
I have big brown eyes, as brown as tree branches.

Naomi Canny (7)
Norland Place School, London

Elliot

E very evening I play fantastic football.
L illa likes lollies.
L aughing lovely Elliot.
I love cold chocolate.
O utside in my garden it is very cold.
T ennis is great.

Elliot Hamilton-Croft (7)
Norland Place School, London

My First Acrostic 2011 - The South

Me

A lexander's favourite
L ollipop flavour is lemon.
E agles are his favourite.
X -rays are not common in his life
A nd he does not like cuts.
N ot that it matters.
D id you know he has a sister?
E lephants are very big.
R abbits are furry.

D eer live in the countryside.
A mphibians can live in water.
V anilla is his favourite
I ce cream flavour.
E lastic is pingy.
S ellotape is for sticking.

Alexander Davies (7)
Norland Place School, London

All About Me

C aspar is a funny person.

A lways loves to play sporty games.

S ometimes I like to solve problems.

P ears are my favourite fruit.

A fter school I love snacks.

R eading is my favourite thing.

P iano lessons that's what I do.

R unning races are fun.

E ating hamburgers is good.

S ummer holidays are my favourite holidays.

S unny Sundays are the best days of the week.

E very day I laugh.

R esponsible I am.

V ery often I play football.

Caspar Presser Velder (7)
Norland Place School, London

Alec Hogarth

A lec and Arun are having a play date today.
L ovely Alec makes lots of friends.
E very day I go to school.
C lever Alec likes maths.

H appy Alec likes to play.
O nly Alec has his own book.
G reedy Alec loves food.
A lec always plays with his friends.
R ude raspberries are fun to blow.
T hink that I have a good mind.
H arry Potter books are best.

Alec Hogarth (7)
Norland Place School, London

Jack Douglas

J ack is as fast as lightning
A nd I like playing
C harlie is as annoying as a monkey
K angaroos knock people's teeth out

D aring ducks get chicken pox
O nly tigers hurt evil rabbits
U nfortunately Indians eat curry
G reat, gosh, it's a dinosaur
L ovely dinosaurs eat flowers
A lways enjoy cookery club
S unny Saturdays are the best.

Jack Douglas (7)
Norland Place School, London

Eva Strage

E va's excellent at French,
V ery intelligent and creative,
A very fine and precious girl,

S neakily she keeps sweets under her bed,
T alented as a monkey,
R eading books is my favourite,
A lways forgetting to do thank you cards,
G reedy with chocolate,
E va loves her bed.

Eva Strage (7)
Norland Place School, London

Arun Mukherjee

A run and his friends like to play
R un Arun, run Alec, you're in a race
U nfortunately I can't play on the Wii
   when my sister is watching TV
N o one loves my teachers better than me

M y toys are very special to me
U nderneath my bed there is a spare bed that I bounce on
K atya and I like to play
H undreds of people love teachers
E verybody loves school
R eading is so fun
J ill loves Arun
'E ating Arun' loves ice cream
E very weekend I play.

Arun Mukherjee (7)
Norland Place School, London

My First Acrostic 2011 - The South

Oscar Jonhede

O scar likes orchestras
S hampoo is shaggy.
C anvas is so soft.
A utumn is freezing.
R eflections are awesome.

J eans are very cool.
O il can make a fire.
N etball is fun.
H alloween is spooky.
E scalators can be useful.
D reams can be scary or nice.
E agles are awesome.

Oscar Jonhede (7)
Norland Place School, London

All About Me

A licia likes creamy hot chocolate.
L eaping Alicia no wonder what I do?
I love ICT, good teacher, good school.
C hicks, yay!
I love cute and cuddly dogs.
A rgh, a rat!

F ish and chips, yum-yum!
E ggs, I cook and read a book.
R ig and a jig, I love to dig.
G et your flowers, I love to smell.
U nderneath my bed a secret place seeks.
S unny Sundays are my favourite.
O ranges ripe and round.
N aughty cat!

Alicia De Broe-Ferguson (7)
Norland Place School, London

My Life

T remendous life can come and peep.
H ilarious times are always sneaking in.
E ncouragement is always with me.
O ne time I remember.

M um said she loves me so much
A t all times.
C arelessly, I don't do things the right way.
K aleidoscopes are very interesting,
E specially on my own.
N ormally I am funny.
Z ebras were my favourite animal.
I ncredible work I do!
E nglish people are in my family or European.

Theo Mackenzie (7)
Norland Place School, London

All About Me

A lex is a funny person
L oves to laugh and play
E ats lots of hamburgers
X ylophone he likes to play

A lso plays games
D odgeball is a funny name
A ssembly ruins it always
M aking it boring for me Mister M calls
S marter me, I am wonderful and tame.

Alex Adams (7)
Norland Place School, London

My First Acrostic 2011 - The South

My Life

J ames is super,
A eroplanes are my favourite,
M ummy is cuddly,
E very day I get annoyed,
S ausages sticking out of mash is my favourite,

W eekends are my favourite time,
A book is brilliant,
R eal James,
D addy is great.

James Ward (7)
Norland Place School, London

Isabella Chen

I sabella is super
S ausages are yummy
A ride on the roller coaster
B allerinas are my favourite things
E verywhere I go I smell the fresh air
L adybirds flutter everywhere
L aughing is fun for me
A rt is my favourite subject

C ake is yummy
H appiness is kind
E ating chocolate is yummy
N etball is what I do in school.

Isabella Chen (6)
Norland Place School, London

My Poem

A melia likes going to fun parties
M ummy likes bony fish
E la is my fast friend
L ive, love, eat!
I like going to the cold park
A melia likes sweets, sweets

P olly is slow
E la is fast
A fter dinner I have a hot bath
R unning is super cool
L essons are great.

Amelia Pearl (7)
Norland Place School, London

All About Me

J ulia likes going in her sparkly car,
U mbrellas are as waterproof as me,
L ollipops are my favourite,
I have a lovely mummy,
A nd a lovely daddy,

B rownies are my favourite,
A lways remember the rules,
L ovely Alicia is my friend,
J ulia enjoys school,
É va is a great friend.

Julia Baljé (7)
Norland Place School, London

My Name

L ovely Lucia
U ntidy at home
C olouring is my favourite
I ce cream is too
A rtistic girl.

Lucia Harrison (6)
Stepping Stones Pre-Preparatory School, Froxfield

My First Acrostic 2011 - The South

My Name

T allulah is my name
A mazing girl
L ovely manners
L ikes playing with Lucia
U nderstands sometimes
L earns lessons
A rchie is my big brother
H appy Hubie is my brother.

Tallulah Mackenzie-Smith (6)
Stepping Stones Pre-Preparatory School, Froxfield

My Name

I ntelligent little girl
S uper Max is my brother
A lways very pretty
B rilliant at reading
E arly morning breakfast club
L ots of cats
L aughs very loudly
A melie is my friend.

Isabella Owen (6)
Stepping Stones Pre-Preparatory School, Froxfield

My Name

A mazing sense of humour
M ischievous little monkey
E xcellent reading all the time
L ovely little girl
I ntelligent and hardworking
E nthusiastic for everything.

Amelie Summers (6)
Stepping Stones Pre-Preparatory School, Froxfield

My Name

I zzy is intelligent
S he is sweet and kind
A mazing at maths
B eautiful big brown eyes
E xcited when it's home time
L ooks forward to the weekend
L oves everybody in her family
A ble to climb the rope.

Isabella Bidwell (5)
Stepping Stones Pre-Preparatory School, Froxfield

My First Acrostic 2011 - The South

My Name

C harlotte is fun
H appy when my mummy is happy
A mazing Mary in the play
R eally excited in the pool
L istens to stories
O nly six
T ries to be good
T ries to be brave
E veryone likes her.

Charlotte Wordsworth (6)
Stepping Stones Pre-Preparatory School, Froxfield

My Name

H appy and noisy
A mazing story writer
R emarkable swimmer
R eally funny sometimes
Y ounger sister called Freya.

Harry Markham (6)
Stepping Stones Pre-Preparatory School, Froxfield

My Name

A mazing, pretty girl
N ever naughty
N ice to people
A lexandra is my sister
B eautiful, pretty manners
E ggs are my favourite
L ovely well-mannered girl.

Annabel Brown (6)
Stepping Stones Pre-Preparatory School, Froxfield

My Name

E xcellent fast worker
D ancing like Strictly
I like instruments
E nthusiastic girl.

Edie Doherty (6)
Stepping Stones Pre-Preparatory School, Froxfield

My Name

P olite and love laughing with others.
A m always kind to my friends.
T oday I play sport.
R eading books is fun.
I am a boy who lives in Axford.
C an play rugby.
K eeping my room tidy is easy.

G ood most of the time.
O n Saturday I get up very early.
O nce I get up I eat breakfast.
D addy has a big boat.
W hen it's nice we go for walks.
I n the summer I go to the beach.
N ever unkind to anyone.

Patrick Goodwin (7)
Stepping Stones Pre-Preparatory School, Froxfield

My Name

J oe is my brother.

A lways riding my bike.

C an do fantastic flips on my skateboard.

K ing Jack is what I want to be.

M y favourite food is chips.

C atching fish with my friends.

N obody can stop me playing on the computer.

A lways silly.

L ikes to play Club Penguin.

L oves war games.

Y esterday I played rugby.

Jack McNally (6)
Stepping Stones Pre-Preparatory School, Froxfield

My First Acrostic 2011 – The South

My Name

J asper likes jam.

A pples are my favourite fruit.

S ometimes I get up at six o'clock.

P lays judo.

E xpert at LEGO.

R unning I like.

F irst thing in the morning I play.

A fter school I eat my supper.

N ext to my teddies is my torch.

S ometimes I like to eat sweets.

H appy and smiley.

A untie Carrie lives a long way away.

W e always have fun at weekends.

E veryone in the class is my friend.

Jasper Fanshawe (7)
Stepping Stones Pre-Preparatory School, Froxfield

My Name

P retty perfect at everything
H appy Phoebe every day
O n Thursday I go swimming
E arly in the morning I eat cereal
B eautiful dress every day
E very day I go to school

F riday is my favourite day
O n school days I read to my teacher
X ylophones are fun
L ovely Mrs Lucas
E verybody is kind
Y asmin is my friend.

Phoebe Foxley (6)
Stepping Stones Pre-Preparatory School, Froxfield

My Name

H appy watching rugby
U sually gets up first
G oalie kicking with my football
O n a Sunday I play rugby

L ove eating burgers
A fter school I play games
W hen my sister plays I do sport
S port is the best
O n a Saturday I play rugby
N ext to my house is a goal.

Hugo Lawson (6)
Stepping Stones Pre-Preparatory School, Froxfield

My Name

On a Saturday I go horse riding.
Lovely food is good to eat.
In the garden I have a rabbit run.
Very often I go to the shops.
In the winter I like playing with the snow.
At school I like doing my work.

Always try to make new friends.
Sometimes I clean the car for my daddy.
Home is my favourite place.
Friends often come to tea with me.
In my bedroom I have a huge teddy bear.
Each day I brush my teeth.
Lively people make me laugh.
Dogs are my favourite pet.

Olivia Ashfield (7)
Stepping Stones Pre-Preparatory School, Froxfield

My First Acrostic 2011 - The South

Dinosaur

D inosaurs are scary
I ncredible claws
N asty teeth
O ld dinosaurs eat meat
S ome dinosaurs are scary
A te little dinosaurs
U ltra little dinosaurs
R eally big.

Kelsey Ashby (5)
Stondon Lower School, Lower Stondon

Dinosaur

D eadly
I n Africa
N asty
O range
S cary, scary
A ngry, angry
U nkind
R oar!

Toby Owen (6)
Stondon Lower School, Lower Stondon

Dinosaur

D aft
I like these
N aughty
O range
S cary
A ngry
U nfriendly
R unning.

Luca La Francesca (5)
Stondon Lower School, Lower Stondon

Dinosaurs

D inosaurs are big
I t has long legs
N o one has seen a dinosaur
O n his fingers are very sharp claws
S cary dinosaur
A small dinosaur runs very fast
U ltra big dinosaurs have very fierce claws
R ed dinosaur is angry.

Cerys Fanning (7)
Stondon Lower School, Lower Stondon

My First Acrostic 2011 - The South

Dinosaur

D angerous

I n Pangea

N aughty because he hurts other dinos

O n the go!

S cratching trees

A ngry

U nder the ground fossils are found

R ipping other dinos.

Dan Taylor (6)
Stondon Lower School, Lower Stondon

Dinosaur

D inosaurs are very fast and small dinosaurs run really fast.

I n Germany and France dinosaurs live.

N ice dinosaurs live.

O mnivore dinosaurs eat vegetables.

S mall dinosaurs.

A ll dinosaurs are in the world.

U p the mountain dinosaur lives.

R un dinosaur fast.

Emily Surtees (6)
Stondon Lower School, Lower Stondon

Dinosaur

D angerous
I like their teeth
N asty
O range
S cary
A ngry
U nkind
R unning.

Cole Sugden
Stondon Lower School, Lower Stondon

Dinosaur

D inosaur
I nvisible T-rex
N ever see a dinosaur
O mnivores are dinosaurs
S ame as a T-rex
A T-rex can rip through a dinosaur
U nderneath T-rex is cool
R exs are like dinosaurs.

Robert Harrison (5)
Stondon Lower School, Lower Stondon

My First Acrostic 2011 - The South

Dinosaurs Poem

D angerous dino
I ncredible
N aughty because they snatch meat
O cean dinosaurs
S caly everywhere
A patosaurus munching plants
U nderground fossils are found
R ipping meat.

Olivia Williamson (6)
Stondon Lower School, Lower Stondon

Massive Dinosaur Poem

D angerous
I n a cave
N asty claws
O pen mouths
S cary
A ngry
U gly
R oar!

Tom Edgecombe (6)
Stondon Lower School, Lower Stondon

Roaring Dinosaurs

D inosaurs
I ncredible dino
N oisy dinosaurs because they sometimes roar
O pen mouths to get small animals
S *nap!* goes its mouth
A patosaurus has the longest neck
U nder the ground are fossils
R oaring.

George Starling (6)
Stondon Lower School, Lower Stondon

Dinosaur

D angerous
I n a cave
N aughty dinosaurs because they eat each other
O pen mouth
S tomping
A ngry dinosaurs
U gly
R oar!

Jessamine Game (6)
Stondon Lower School, Lower Stondon

My First Acrostic 2011 - The South

Dinosaurs

D aft dinosaur.
I ncredibly tall tail.
N ot kind.
O ften fierce.
S o scary.
A scary dinosaur.
U nder a tree.
R eally red!

Ashleigh Fenton (5)
Stondon Lower School, Lower Stondon

Dinosaurs

D inosaurs are scary, they are crazy.
I ncredible and they are scary.
N ice, dinosaurs are nice.
O mnivores only eat meat!
S ome dinosaurs are little.
A dinosaur.
U nbelievably sharp teeth.
R oar!

Surena Kumar (6)
Stondon Lower School, Lower Stondon

Dinosaurs

D inosaurs are fast
I like dinosaurs
N ice dinosaurs jump
O nly dinosaurs
S harp teeth
A carnivore
U gly dinosaur
R oar now dinosaur.

Kiera Marlow (6)
Stondon Lower School, Lower Stondon

Nabilah

N ever lets anyone down.
A lways kind to others.
B eautiful as always.
I ntelligent and incredible.
L ikes helping others.
A bright and talented girl.
H as a good sense of humour.

Nabilah Ibrahim (7)
Whitefield Infant School, Luton

I Like My Burger

I like chicken burgers

L ovely burger
I t is a fantastic burger
K etchup in my burger
E xcellent burger

M y mum cooks burgers for me
Y ummy scrummy in my tummy

B urger buns
U nbelievably amazing burger
R ayhan likes burgers
G reat, brilliant burger
E atable burger
R eally, really good burger.

Rayhan Ahmed (6)
Whitefield Infant School, Luton

Summer Holidays

S un, sand and sea is where I wish to be
U mbrellas are not used for me
M y family like fun times in the sun
M ummy spends special times with me
E ating lots of ice cream and lollies
R ain can stay away for my special time

H appy holidays
O range juice is refreshing for me
L iving in a caravan for a week
I love this time for me
D ays go past
A pples grow on tall trees
Y oghurt
S uncream, lots will do.

Lauren Matear (7)
Whitefield Infant School, Luton

My First Acrostic

R acing Ryan.
Y oung boy.
A mazing footballer.
N ice boy.

C harming young boy.
H igh jumper.
I ce cream boy.
L ively boy.
V ehicle loves driving.
E nergetic.
R ide my bike.
S trong boy.

Ryan Chilvers (7)
Whitefield Infant School, Luton

Ashleigh

A nt who is a creature

S nake who really is slimy

H ippo who is heavy and dirty

L ion who is furry

E xcellent which means very good or outstanding

I njection which is a needle in the arm

G ames that you can play

H airdresser that cuts your hair.

Ashleigh Ridlington (6)
Whitefield Infant School, Luton

My First Acrostic 2011 - The South

Young Writers Information

We hope you have enjoyed reading this book - and that you will continue to enjoy it in the coming years.

If you like reading and writing poetry drop us a line, or give us a call, and we'll send you a free information pack.

Alternatively if you would like to order further copies of this book or any of our other titles, then please give us a call or log onto our website at www.youngwriters.co.uk.

Young Writers Information
Remus House
Coltsfoot Drive
Peterborough
PE2 9BF
(01733) 890066